ESPECIALLY FOR

_____

FROM

_____

DATE

_____

A CELEBRATION
OF GOD'S LOVE

A Keepsake Devotional Featuring the
Inspirational Verse of Helen Steiner Rice

BARBOUR
PUBLISHING

A HELEN STEINER RICE ® Product

Member of the
Evangelical Christian
Publishers Association

Printed in China.

Contents

INTRODUCTION

God's love—how rich and pure and utterly amazing it is. Our great Creator, almighty God, looks down on us and chooses to see us with loving eyes, call us His children, and redeem us by His grace. We may never understand it; but we can accept and celebrate it.

That's exactly what this book is designed to do. As you read through its pages, we pray you will be blessed and inspired by the beautiful and insightful poetry of Helen Steiner Rice. Each poem has been coupled with a devotional thought designed to draw you into a glorious celebration of God's love. It is your highest calling, what you were born to do. Allow yourself to be caught up in it, exploring both the grandeur and the practical nature of it all.

God bless you as we celebrate God's love together.

God's Love

God's love is like an island in life's ocean vast and wide—
A peaceful, quiet shelter from the restless, rising tide.
God's love is like an anchor when the angry billows roll—
A mooring in the storms of life, a stronghold for the soul.
God's love is like a fortress, and we seek protection there
When the waves of tribulation seem to drown us in despair.
God's love is like a harbor where our souls can find sweet rest
From the struggle and the tension of life's fast and futile quest.
God's love is like a beacon burning bright with faith and prayer,
And through the changing scenes of life, we can find a haven there.

~HSR

Celebrating the
Gift of God's Love

God Loves Us

We are all God's children
And He loves us, every one.
He freely and completely
Forgives all that we have done,
Asking only if we're ready
To follow where He leads,
Content that in His wisdom
He will answer all our needs.

~HSR

The Meaning of Love

*This is love: not that we loved God, but that he loved us
and sent his Son as an atoning sacrifice for our sins.*

1 JOHN 4:10 NIV

If we were to put all the world's languages together, there
would be literally hundreds of definitions for the word "love."
In every culture known to us, love is used to express everything
from carnal lust to favorite foods! It has been packaged with
teenage crushes, illicit affairs, casual cravings, and enchantment
with material things.

But real love is something quite different from all this. The
Bible uses the word *love* to describe how God feels about us
and how those loving feelings caused Him to take action. God's
first love-gift to us was the creation of a world so vast, filled
with such variety and beauty and mind-boggling detail, that we
cannot fully comprehend it—a gift that blesses us daily!

The wonder of God's love through nature, however, can
never come close to the love He expressed in sending His only
Son—not only to save our lives but to give us abundant life
when we had no way to gain it on our own.

God's love is never transient, fickle, casual, or changing. It
infuses good marriages, happy families, and lasting friendships.
Most importantly, it is the foundation and lifeblood of our
relationship with Him. If you have never known it, go to the
Source. Your heavenly Father longs to lavish His love on you!

What More Can You Ask?

God's presence is ever beside you,
as near as the reach of your hand.
You have but to tell Him your troubles—
there is nothing He won't understand. . .
And knowing God's love is unfailing,
and His mercy unending and great,
You have but to trust in His promise,
"God comes not too soon or too late". . .
So wait with a heart that is patient
for the goodness of God to prevail,
For never do prayers go unanswered,
and His mercy and love never fail.

~HSR

The Qualities of Love

The Word became flesh and dwelt among us,
and we have seen his glory.

JOHN 1:14 ESV

When love is present, it shows. You can see it in a tender smile and gentle touch, in a willingness to listen, and in a readiness to help. You cannot mistake its presence in the way a loving mother holds her child to her breast, in the way good friends laugh and talk together, in the way a long-married couple holds hands without saying a word.

God's love for you shows, too. You sense it when He lifts your fears and covers you with His comfort. You see it in the faces of your loved ones, you feel it in their embrace, and you hear it in their words of friendship and caring. You experience it when you find within yourself strength to overcome a challenge, and you rejoice in it as you give thanks to Him for the many blessings He has poured into your life.

So His love could be clearly recognized, God sent His Son Jesus to bring you into His family and to make you His child forever. His birth on earth, His death on the cross, and His resurrection from the tomb are all sure signs of God's abiding love.

Spend a few moments thinking about the special ways you can see the signs of God's love for you—love that will last forever.

Beyond Our Asking

More than hearts can imagine
or minds comprehend,
God's bountiful gifts are ours without end.
We ask for a cupful when the vast sea is ours,
We pick a small rosebud from a garden of flowers,
We reach for a sunbeam but the sun still abides,
We draw one short breath
but there's air on all sides.
Whatever we ask for falls short of God's giving,
For His greatness exceeds every facet of living
And always God's ready and eager and willing
To pour out His mercy, completely fulfilling
All of man's needs for peace, joy, and rest,
For God gives His children whatever is best.
Just give Him a chance to open His treasures,
And He'll fill your life with
unfathomable pleasures—
Pleasures that never grow worn out and faded
And leave us depleted, disillusioned and jaded—
For God has a storehouse just filled to the brim
With all that man needs, if we'll only ask Him.

~HSR

The Fullness of Love

Let us then approach the throne of grace with confidence,
so that we may receive mercy and find grace
to help us in our time of need.

HEBREWS 4:16 NIV

"How high is the sky?" If you've ever had a toddler ask you that question, you probably had a tough time coming up with a good answer. You can imagine, then, how this question must sound to God: "How big is Your love?" There's not a good answer, because the height, depth, breadth, and width of God's love far exceed human understanding.

God's feelings for you remain the same, no matter how many times you may have failed to follow His will in thought, word, or action. There's no upper limit to the number of times you can turn to Him and receive His forgiveness, and there's no cutoff point where He will turn you away from His presence. Where even the strongest and deepest human love may have its boundaries and conditions, God's love remains immeasurable, unshakable, and complete.

If you have ever hesitated to come before God's throne for any reason, remember that He sent His son to assure you of His love. Let His Spirit bring you to Him, and kneel before Him in trust and confidence. He welcomes you with a love so big, so marvelous, it's indescribable. All you need to know is this: God's love is there for you today and always.

Enfolded in His Love

The love of God surrounds us
Like the air we breathe around us,
As near as a heartbeat, as close as a prayer,
And whenever we need Him, He'll always be there!

~HSR

The Presence of Love

I'm living and breathing among you right now.

HAGGAI 2:5 MSG

How aware are you of the air you breathe? Most of the time, you probably aren't thinking about it at all. When you wake up, you assume it's going to be there, and when you go to bed, you don't worry about the supply of air running out at night. Under normal circumstances, air is something all of us take for granted!

God's presence is like the air around you—it's always there, whether you're aware of it or not. He is with you as you read this now, just as He is with you when you're standing in the grocery checkout line, walking through your neighborhood, or sitting in your favorite chair at home.

When things are going smoothly, you may not even think at all about God's being there with you. When trials come, however, fear can hide His presence from your eyes. The fog of fear can make you believe He is gone, yet He remains as near to you as the air you breathe.

At these times especially, reach out to Him in prayer, asking the Holy Spirit to lift your anxieties and bathe you in the freshening, strengthening, and comforting presence of your heavenly Father. He will never leave you. God is always there for you.

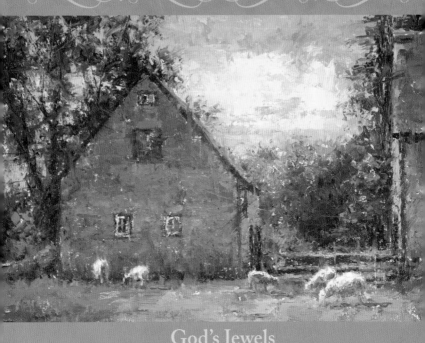

God's Jewels

We watch the rich and famous bedecked in precious jewels,
Enjoying earthly pleasures, defying moral rules,
And in our mood of discontent we sink into despair
And long for earthly riches and feel cheated of our share. . .
But stop these idle musings, God has stored up for you
Treasures that are far beyond earth's jewels and riches, too.
For never, never discount what God has promised man
If he will walk in meekness and accept God's flawless plan.
For if we heed His teaching as we journey through the years,
We'll find the richest jewels of all are crystallized from tears.

~HSR

The Riches of Love

LUKE 12:34 NKJV

If we don't see them all around us, we see them on television—people who seem to have so much more than we do! They buy expensive clothes from designer boutiques while we balk at the price of a sweater at the local department store. They go on exotic vacations while we count our pennies to save up for a weekend away. It doesn't seem fair, does it?

Feelings of discontent come to everyone from time to time. When you are bothered by these thoughts, God invites you to bring your concerns to Him. It's okay to tell Him exactly what you believe you are missing, and to be specific about what is causing you so much unhappiness. Then let go of these things, and let God's Spirit take over.

The Holy Spirit has the power to open your eyes to the riches God has poured on you. In Him, you are robed in saving faith, covered with His promises, and adorned with an eternal relationship with your heavenly Father. Even the wealthiest people in the world could not buy this for themselves! But to you it has been freely given, because God chose to lavish on you the riches of His love—your true and lasting treasure.

Gifts from God

This brings you a million good wishes and more
For the things you cannot buy in a store—
Life faith to sustain you in times of trial,
A joy-filled heart and a happy smile,
Contentment, inner peace, and love—
All priceless gifts from God above!

~HSR

The Gifts of Love

Freely you have received, freely give.

MATTHEW 10:8 NIV

"Money can't buy happiness." It's a cliché, but it's true, isn't it? No doubt you have lived long enough to know that real happiness comes in the form of strong, healthy relationships; fulfilling activity; and a quiet, contented heart.

Here's where God comes in. He desires true happiness for you, and so He makes it possible for you to have it. First, He sends people into your life for you to love and care for, and to love and care for you in return. Second, He gives your life meaning and purpose. No matter what your circumstances may be, He has a plan for you and a reason for your every day.

Third, and most important, God's plan for your present and eternal happiness is found in the life and work of His Son Jesus. Because He fulfilled His Father's will, Jesus earned the peace of mind you have in knowing your sins are forgiven and your future with Him is assured. Now this is more than happiness; it's cause for heartfelt and heart-deep joy!

Your smile, your confidence, and your serenity are all gifts you could never buy anywhere, but only receive and embrace with gratitude, thanks to your loving, gracious, and generous God.

*Celebrating the
Blessings of
God's Love*

Blessings Devised by God

God speaks to us in many ways,
Altering our lives, our plans, and our days,
And His blessings come in many guises
That He alone in love devises,
And sorrow, which we dread so much,
Can bring a very healing touch. . .
For when we fail to heed His voice
We leave the Lord no other choice
Except to use a firm, stern hand
To make us know He's in command. . .
For on the wings of loss and pain,
The peace we often sought in vain
Will come to us with sweet surprise,
For God is merciful and wise. . .
And through dark hours of tribulation
God gives us time for meditation,
And nothing can be counted loss
Which teaches us to bear our cross.

~HSR

The Lessons of Love

It's the child he loves that God corrects;
a father's delight is behind all this.

PROVERBS 3:12 MSG

When we graduate from school as young adults, we might
think we're done with learning. It doesn't take long for us to
realize we've just begun! Throughout life, we learn new ways of
doing things, delve into new subjects, and discover new ideas.
Many of us call ourselves lifelong learners.

In God's school, each one of us is a lifelong learner. No
matter how old we are, not one of us can truthfully say we
know all we need to know about God's commandments, His
Word, or His will. Throughout life, we will stray, we will wander
away from Him, and then we will find ourselves right back in
front of our Teacher, learners once again. We will never graduate from needing God's correction and guidance, His mercy
and forgiveness, until we are standing face to face with Him in
heaven.

If you are bearing the consequences of a mistake you have
made, thank God. Thank God, because He cares so much about
you that He continues to teach you how to live according to
His plan for your life. Thank Him for bringing you to this day,
because you have the privilege of rejoicing in His unchangeable
truths, gaining spiritual wisdom, and, through your example,
teaching others about His love.

Showers of Blessings

Each day there are showers of blessings
sent from the Father above,
For God is a great, lavish giver,
and there is no end to His love. . .
And His grace is more than sufficient,
His mercy is boundless and deep,
And His infinite blessings are countless,
and all this we're given to keep
If we but seek God and find Him
and ask for a bounteous measure
Of this wholly immeasurable offering
from God's inexhaustible treasure. . .
For no matter how big man's dreams are,
God's blessings are infinitely more,
For always God's giving is greater
than what man is asking for.

~HSR

The Greatness of Love

I will send down showers in season;
there will be showers of blessing.

EZEKIEL 34:26 NIV

What is the most amazing thing that has happened during
your lifetime so far? Perhaps you were awed when Neil
Armstrong set foot on the moon in 1969; when Dr. Robert
Jarvik implanted the first artificial heart in 1982; when you
realized you could talk to anyone, anywhere, on a device no
larger than the palm of your hand! These and others advances
in medicine and technology happened and continue to happen
because people use the power of their imaginations and put
them to work.

When we attempt to describe what God is like, however,
the power of our imagination falls woefully short. That's
because, no matter how big our idea may be, we cannot begin
to grasp His limitless love or His infinite power. When we try,
we limit our ability to reach out as far as He would have us
reach, to believe in the blessings He has in mind for us, and
to recognize all the opportunities He has placed right in front
of us.

God invites you to ask Him for whatever you can dream,
then let Him take care of the rest. His imagination and power
are far greater than anything you could think of, so prepare
to be amazed at how much more your heavenly Father will
choose to shower on you!

The Magic of Love

Love is like magic and it always will be,
For love still remains life's sweet mystery.
Love works in ways that are wondrous and strange,
And there's nothing in life that love cannot change.
Love can transform the most commonplace
Into beauty and splendor and sweetness and grace.
Love is unselfish, understanding, and kind,
For it sees with its heart and not with its mind.
Love gives and forgives; there is nothing too much
For love to heal with its magic touch.
Love is the language that every heart speaks,
For love is the one thing that every heart seeks. . .
And where there is love God, too, will abide
And bless the family residing inside.

~HSR

The Transformation of Love

By this we know that we abide in him and he in us,
because he has given us of his Spirit.

1 JOHN 4:13 ESV

When we're in love, the world is transformed. There's a spring to our step and a lilt to our voice, and we notice things we've never noticed before, like how beautifully the moon shines and how brightly the birds sing. We find ourselves making new plans and envisioning new possibilities. Without doubt, love changes things!

God's love changes things, too. In fact, He changes us! Rather than leave us separated from Him because of our sin, God loved us so much He sent His Son Jesus to repair and renew our relationship with Him. He literally transformed us from sinners to saints! To keep us close to Him, God sent His Holy Spirit to live within our hearts so we could grow in His love, mature in His love, and act on His love.

Yes, God's love will change the way you see the world. You will see wonders and miracles; you will discover purpose, fulfillment, and joy; and you will receive an abundance of blessings.

The kindness and mercy, patience and thoughtfulness, and care and concern you show for others are sure signs of transformation taking place. They're just a few of the ways you know that God's world-changing love is at work in your life and His Spirit is at home in your heart.

God Bless You and Keep You in His Care

There are many things in life
we cannot understand,
But we must trust God's judgment
and be guided by His hand. . .
And all who have God's blessing
can rest safely in His care,
For He promises safe passage
on the wings of faith and prayer.

~HSR

The Promise of Love

He will command his angels concerning you
to guard you in all your ways;
they will lift you up in their hands,
so that you will not strike your foot against a stone.

PSALM 91:11–12 NIV

"God has not promised a smooth ride, but He has promised a safe landing." Perhaps you've seen these words posted on a church sign or bulletin board. They're good words to remember when disappointment strikes, when it seems things aren't working out for you, when the road ahead looks anything but smooth.

During life's bumpy rides, God would have us remember that these times are only temporary, and that they are part of His perfect plan for us. He keeps us from falling into despair and hopelessness by assuring us He knows and cares about our circumstances, our fears, and our feelings.

By enabling you to look beyond today and into eternity, God gives you the strength and courage you need to keep believing in Him and trusting in His promises. What you're going through may make no sense to you right now, but at the end you will know and you will rejoice.

In troubled times especially, God invites you to lean on Him. Approach Him in faith, speak to Him about your needs, and rely on Him to help you over the pitfalls and potholes that lie before you. Let Him lift you up and bring you to a safe landing now and to eternity.

Look on the Sunny Side

There are always two sides—the good and the bad,
The dark and the light, the sad and the glad. . .
But in looking back over the good and the bad,
We're aware of the number of good things we've had,
And in counting our blessings, we find when we're through
We've no reason at all to complain or be blue. . .
So thank God for the good things He has already done,
And be grateful to Him for the battles you've won,
And know that the same God who helped you before
Is ready and willing to help you once more,
Then with faith in your heart, reach out for God's hand
And accept what He sends, though you can't understand. . .
For our Father in heaven always knows what is best,
And if you trust His wisdom, your life will be blessed. . .
For always remember that whatever betide you,
You are never alone, for God is beside you.

~HSR

The Legacy of Love

Bless the LORD, O my soul,
and forget not all His benefits.

PSALM 103:2 NKJV

Imagine you are paging through an old family photo album
or scrapbook. In it, you find pictures of yourself when you
were born, when you took your first steps, and when you first
started school. Pictures of the place where you used to live; of
your family and friends; of your graduations, celebrations, and
birthday parties remind you of all the ways you've changed,
grown, and matured throughout the years.

An album like this—real or imaginary—also serves to
remind you of how God has taken care of you from the time
you were born right up to this day. In your mind, try to picture
all the good things He has brought into your life, and let your
heart swell in praise and gratitude! See if you can count all the
times He has delivered you from danger, relieved your fears,
and comforted you in your sorrows! Are not these reasons to
feel good about what your Lord has done in your life?

God invites you to confidently put your trust in Him now
and place the future in His hands. You know how He has kept
you in the past, and He has both the desire and the power to
protect you, comfort you, and bless you today and every day to
come.

Be Glad

Be glad that your life has
been full and complete,
Be glad that you've tasted
the bitter and sweet.
Be glad that you've walked
in sunshine and rain,
Be glad that you've felt
both pleasure and pain.
Be glad that you've had such
a full, happy life,
Be glad for your joy as
well as your strife.
Be glad that you've walked
with courage each day,
Be glad you've had strength
for each step of the way.
Be glad for the comfort
that you've found in prayer.
Be glad for God's blessings,
His love, and His care.

~HSR

The Pattern of Love

Known to God from eternity are all His works.

ACTS 15:18 NKJV

If you have ever put together or admired a patchwork quilt, you know that its beauty rests in its varied colors and patterns. You see bold colors contrasting with soft colors, simple fabric patterns alternating with complex prints, plaids, and stripes. Through skillful use of colors and patterns of fabric, the artist creates a quilt of texture, depth, and beauty.

Your life, similar to a patchwork quilt, is made up of dark and light moments, and simple and complex emotions. A time you learned a hard lesson may lie alongside a time your wisdom guided someone else. A time you drew back in fear may be surrounded by times you acted with courage and boldness. All these things were necessary to give you the knowledge, experience, and spiritual beauty you now possess.

But unlike a patchwork quilt, which you can admire from edge to edge, you cannot yet look at the span of your life and see all the colors, patterns, and designs yet to be added. Only God, the Master Artist, can do that! But you can survey your life so far with gladness and satisfaction, and with the certainty that He knows all about you, He delights in you—and He's not finished with you yet!

God's Keeping

To be in God's keeping is surely a blessing,
For though life is often dark and distressing,
No day is too dark and no burden too great
That God in His love cannot penetrate.

~HSR

The Light of Love

"I am the light of the world. The person who follows me will never live in darkness but will have the light that gives life."

JOHN 8:12 NCV

When evening comes, the first thing we might do is flick on a lamp or light a candle. As darkness falls around us, our light glows even brighter, and with it we can see our way through the night.

God's love is like a light that glows in the darkness of our fears and anxieties. Through the saving work of His Son Jesus, God has poured out on us the cleansing light of forgiveness and the assurance of salvation. Through the work of the Holy Spirit in our hearts, God shines on us the renewing light that shatters the darkness of despair and hopelessness. Through the words of scripture, our heavenly Father guides us through all the shadowy passages of life and brings us safely to the dawn of a new day.

As you receive and accept the light of His love, you shine as a light of hope to loved ones and friends who are standing in darkness, wondering which way to go. Your words of comfort and encouragement will lessen their heavy burden, and your prayers on their behalf work to penetrate their doubts and fears.

Like the flame of a candle, the light of your faith shines brightest in the darkest of night. Let it shine, let it shine, let it shine!

Celebrating the
Power of
God's Love

God's Love Is a Haven
in the Storms of Life

God's love is like an island in life's ocean vast and wide,
A peaceful, quiet shelter from the restless, rising tide.
God's love is like a fortress, and we seek protection there
When the waves of tribulation seem to drown us in despair.
God's love is a sanctuary where our souls can find sweet rest
From the struggle and the tension of life's fast and futile quest.
God's love is like a tower rising far above the crowd,
And God's smile is like the sunshine
breaking through the threatening cloud.
God's love is like a beacon burning bright
with faith and prayer,
And through all the changing scenes of life
we can find a haven there.
For God's love is fashioned after something enduring
And it is endless and unfailing like His character above.

~HSR

The Haven of Love

God is our refuge and strength,
a very present help in trouble.
PSALM 46:1 NKJV

Where do you go when you need a few minutes' time out?
Perhaps you retire to your bedroom and shut the door, or sit
outside in the calming quietness of your garden. Wherever you
choose, you're looking for a place of temporary haven from the
tumult and troubles of life. It's a place you can be by yourself to
relax your body and refresh your mind.

In His love, God opens His arms as your spiritual haven,
inviting you to come to Him whenever you need "time out"
from the problems that surround you. No, He does not promise
an escape from your troubles, but He does promise to strengthen
and comfort you. He promises to listen to your worries and
to send His Holy Spirit into your heart to renew your faith,
your confidence, and your ability to carry on.

In the haven of God's love, He offers you an opportunity
to step aside and see your problems from another perspective.
Time alone with God allows Him to counsel you, and He opens
your heart and soul to receive His wisdom and inspiration.

Today, take a few minutes' time out with God. Find your
haven from your fears and anxieties in Him, because in Him is
your comfort, strength, and peace.

The Way to Love and Peace

Let us recognize we're facing problems
man has never solved,
And with all our daily efforts life grows
more and more involved...
But our future will seem brighter
and we'll meet with less resistance
If we call upon our Father and seek divine assistance,
For the spirit can unravel many tangled, knotted threads
That defy the skill and power
of the world's best hands and heads,
And our plans for growth and progress,
of which we all have dreamed,
Cannot survive materially
unless our spirits are redeemed...
For only when the mind of man
is united with the soul
Can love and peace combine to make
our lives complete and whole.

~HSR

The Strength of Love

"I fill all of heaven and earth," says the LORD.

JEREMIAH 23:24 NCV

"Where is God?" It's a natural question when we're overwhelmed by tragedy. It can be a personal tragedy, such as terminal illness or an untimely death; or it can be a national tragedy, such as our recent economic recession; or a global tragedy, such as wars between countries. Where is God in all this?

God would answer, "Right here with you, where I've always been." We fail to notice Him because we believe we're suffering something way too big for God to change, way too heavy for God to handle, so we don't involve Him. When He doesn't intervene in the way we think He should, we conclude God doesn't have the strength, power, or interest to do anything.

Our God, who was there when His beloved Son Jesus suffered and died on the cross for us, is the same God who can and will carry the burden of our sorrows. Jesus' victory over death proves that even our worst tragedy, death, is no match for God, who invites us to lay all our fears at the foot of His throne.

Where is God in your personal tragedies and in the world's terrors? Right there with you! Let the eyes of your spirit see Him as He opens His arms of comfort and reassurance to you in all life's circumstances.

Great Faith that Smiles
Are Born of Great Trials

It's easy to say "In God we trust"
when life is radiant and fair,
But the test of faith is only found
when there are burdens to bear. . .
For our claim to faith in the
sunshine is really no faith at all,
For when roads are smooth and days
are bright our need for God is so small. . .
And no one discovers the fullness
or the greatness of God's love
Unless they have walked in the darkness
with only a light from above. . .
For the faith to endure whatever
comes is born of sorrow and trials
And strengthened only by discipline
and nurtured by self-denials. . .
So be not disheartened by troubles,
for trials are the building blocks
On which to erect a fortress of faith,
secure on God's ageless rocks.

~HSR

The Test of Love

We consider blessed those who have persevered.

JAMES 5:11 NIV

Few schoolchildren look forward to tests! They worry how well they will do, and they fear seeing questions they are not prepared to answer. Yet teachers don't give tests to instill anxiety, but to find out if their students have grasped the material they have been taught.

In the same way, God permits tests of love, faith, and commitment to come into our lives not to threaten us, but to teach us something about ourselves. Suppose we're falling into despair because we're having a hard time right now, or finding ourselves tempted by the same old sin again and again. How do we respond?

This is a time to remember what God has taught us! We recall His saving work of love and forgiveness through the life, death, and resurrection of His Son Jesus, and we bring to mind His repeated promises of His constant presence and marvelous power. We picture in our mind's eye His open arms, and we hear His words of invitation to bring our cares and concerns to Him in prayer.

Though God is aware of the strength of your love, faith, and commitment to Him, you are not, unless these things are tested. Ask Him to give you everything you need to pass each test with flying colors!

Put Your Problems in God's Hands
for He Completely Understands

Although it sometimes seems to us our prayers have not been heard,
God always knows our every need without a single word,
And He will not forsake us even though the way is steep,
For always He is near to us, a tender watch to keep...
And in good time He will answer us, and in His love He'll send
Greater things than we have asked and blessings without end...
So though we do not understand why trouble comes to man,
Can we not be contented just to know it is God's plan?

~HSR

The Freedom of Love

Cast all your anxiety on him
because he cares for you.

1 PETER 5:7 NIV

A friend has something on her mind, so you sit with her in a quiet place and ask her about it. Tearfully, she explains her dilemma. But before you can say anything or offer your help, she leaves, taking her anguish along with her.

We do the same thing when we bring our burdens to God, then pick them right up again. We do it when we deliver our sins to the foot of His cross, then continue to bear the weight of our guilt, and when we ask for God's help, but insist on solving our problems in our own way.

In the life and ministry of Jesus, God's Son, we see God's mercy, compassion, and power at work in the lives of people— people with devastating sicknesses and people with little to hope for. He healed them! He delivered them! He died on the cross and rose again to show us His victory over our most deadly problem, sin. He took the guilt of our sin on His shoulders! It's gone!

Gather up everything that weighs on your heart, and carry the load to your heavenly Father and place it at His feet. Humbly accept His words of forgiveness, then walk away, arms free and heart at peace. This is His love at work in you.

Meet Life's Trials with Smiles

There are times when life overwhelms us
and our trials seem too many to bear.
It is then we should stop to remember
God is standing by ready to share
The uncertain hours that confront us
and fill us with fear and despair,
For God in His goodness has promised
that the cross that He gives us to wear
Will never exceed our endurance or be
more than our strength can bear. . .
And secure in that blessed assurance,
we can smile as we face tomorrow,
For God holds the key to the future,
and no sorrow or care we need borrow.

~HSR

The Assurance of Love

Whoever does not take his cross and
follow me is not worthy of me.

MATTHEW 10:38 ESV

Athletes, if they are serious about competing and winning, need to keep challenging themselves. After they complete one level of training, they eagerly take on the next, firmly confident that they will master this one, too. Without firm belief in their ability, however, they would quickly lose heart and stop trying.

Throughout life, we experience challenges, many of them serious, even devastating. Yet despite what happens, it's our firm confidence in God's power to provide us with the strength we need to triumph that achieves our victory. The more we experience His work in our lives, the more we rely on Him and the more our faith in His strength grows.

God permits problems to come into your life for a reason, and often it's so He can show you how strong you are when you lean on Him. It's His way of keeping you from avoiding challenges and weakening in the face of fear. The cross He gives you to bear is one He knows you can carry, because through Jesus' saving work, He has proven His victory over the troubles of this world.

Your cross is just one more sign of the strength and power you have in Him, a cross you're not carrying alone. You have the assurance of the power of His continuing love.

Somebody Loves You

Somebody loves you more than you know,
Somebody goes with you wherever you go,
Somebody really and truly cares
And lovingly listens to all of your prayers. . .
Don't think for a minute that this is not true,
For God loves His children and takes care of them, too. . .
And all of His treasures are yours to share
If you love Him completely and show that you care. . .
And if you walk in His footsteps and have faith to believe,
There's nothing you ask for that you will not receive!

~HSR

The Friendship of Love

I've named you friends.
JOHN 15:15 MSG

Having caring people around us has been compared to having food on the table—it's essential to our mental and physical health. Just as food provides the nutrients our body needs to function, so our friends, family, and loved ones play a vital role in our spiritual well-being, as we do in theirs.

At some point in life, however, we may find ourselves suffering from loneliness and the heaviness of heart it brings. Perhaps we have moved to a new town, or a loved one has passed away. That's when God's promise to be with us at all times soothes the soul and gives solace in the silent hours. Just knowing we are never truly alone lifts the weight of loneliness from us and opens us to His comforting embrace.

Jesus is your forever friend, and no matter where you are, He is by your side. With your companionship in Him, reach out to others with your friendship, care, and concern. Listen to them as your Lord listens to you, and offer to them the words of love and encouragement you have heard from Him.

When you do your part to lift the weight of loneliness from the hearts of others, you keep its burden far, far away from your own!

Celebrating Our Thankfulness for God's Love

So Many Reasons to Love the Lord

Thank You, God, for little things that come unexpectedly
To brighten up a dreary day that dawned so dismally.
Thank You, God, for sending a happy thought my way
To blot out my depression on a disappointing day.
Thank You, God, for brushing the dark clouds from my mind
And leaving only sunshine and joy of heart behind.
Oh God, the list is endless of the things to thank You for,
But I take them all for granted and unconsciously ignore
That everything I think or do, each movement that I make,
Each measured, rhythmic heartbeat, each breath of life I take
Is something You have given me for which there is no way
For me in all my smallness to in any way repay.

~HSR

The Response of Love

How great are your works,
O Lord, how profound your thoughts!
PSALM 92:5 NIV

You give unselfishly when you give to someone who cannot pay you back. When you help a needy person, you're not looking for a reward or a favor in return; you respond simply because you see a need and you have it in your heart to fill it.

The blessings God generously showers on you every day are signs of the love He has in His heart for you. When someone comes along at just the right time to say hello, to cheer you up, or to help you out, it's because God saw your need and He filled it. When an unexpected joy comes into your life, it's because God desires to specially bless you, so He does.

Is there a favor you can do for Him in return? Can you ever hope to repay Him? No, your heavenly Father has everything, and He has done everything for you. His Son Jesus has completely taken care of the question of your relationship with God, your complete innocence in His eyes, and your eternal life with Him.

The only response left for you is the same one you hope a needy person you bless with your giving will have—to pass on the goodness, the kindness, and the heartfelt love to the next person.

Thank You, God, for Everything

Thank You, God, for everything—the big things and the small—
For every good gift comes from God, the Giver of them all,
And all too often we accept without any thanks or praise
The gifts God sends as blessings each day in many ways.
And so at this time we offer up a prayer
To thank You, God, for giving us a lot more than our share.
First, thank You for the little things that often come our way—
The things we take for granted and don't mention when we pray—
The unexpected courtesy, the thoughtful, kindly deed,
A hand reached out to help us in the time of sudden need.
Oh make us more aware, dear God, of little daily graces
That come to us with sweet surprise from never-dreamed-of places.
Then thank You for the miracles we are much too blind to see,
And give us new awareness of our many gifts from Thee.
And help us to remember that the key to life and living
Is to make each prayer a prayer of thanks and
each day a day of thanksgiving.

~HSR

The Gratitude of Love

In everything give thanks;
for this is the will of God in Christ Jesus for you.

1 Thessalonians 5:18 nkjv

More and more, we're becoming aware of the importance of a life in balance. Experts impress on us the mental and physical health benefits of balancing work and recreation, activity and meditation, exercise and rest. In practice, however, most of us neglect one or two aspects of an ideally balanced life because we're focused on what we feel is most important at the moment.

Similarly, our prayer life gets out of balance when we fill it with our desires and forget about our gratitude. Sometimes our list of requests takes up so much of our prayer time that we never get around to expressing our thanks for everything God has already given us! Sound familiar?

Jesus' sacrifice on the cross assures us of forgiveness for our forgetfulness, as for all other good things we have failed to say or do. To keep us more mindful of His gifts, God sends His Holy Spirit into our hearts to help us know how to pray the kind of prayer God desires to hear.

Keep your prayer life in balance by expressing your praise, revealing your sins and weaknesses, receiving His forgiveness, responding with your gratitude, and then presenting the desires of your heart. With these things in mind, come before your God every day in confidence and joy!

Things to Be Thankful For

The good, green earth beneath our feet,
The air we breathe, the food we eat,
Some work to do, a goal to win,
A hidden longing deep within
That spurs us on to bigger things
And helps us meet what each day brings—
All these things and many more
Are things we should be thankful for. . .
And most of all, our thankful prayers
Should rise to God because He cares.

~HSR

The Wonders of Love

God saw all that he had made, and it was very good.

GENESIS 1:31 NIV

A shaft of sunlight streaming in your window. . .the colors of a rainbow spanning the sky after an afternoon shower. . .a tree heavy with sweet ripe fruit. . .a majestic sunset turning the horizon a glorious red and gold.

All these things are blessings from God to you, and to everyone else, believer and nonbeliever alike. God makes no distinction when it comes to showering people with His abundant gifts! But there is a difference in the response of those who receive His gifts.

The unbeliever, even when looking out over an awe-inspiring vista, or spellbound at the foot of a towering water-fall, does not know whom to thank. He may appreciate it, he may treasure the memory as long as he lives, yet he does not know who formed it. He may love creation, but does not recognize the Creator.

God has planted His Spirit in your heart, enabling you to see the Creator in His creation. The wonders of nature fill you not only with awe, but with thanks to God, who called these things into being at the beginning of time.

You have the benefit of sunshine and starlight, marvels and mysteries, joy and beauty all around you. And even more important, you know whom to thank!

Thoughts of Thanks

At this time may God grant you
Special gifts of joy and cheer,
And bless you for the good you do
For others through the year. . .
May you find rich satisfaction
In your daily work and prayer,
And in knowing as you serve Him
He will keep you in His care.

~HSR

The Truth of Love

The Lord bless you and keep you.

NUMBERS 6:24 NKJV

The best and warmest of wishes are simply sweet sentiments unless they're based in truth. And when they are, they're more than wishes—they're certainties.

Because God, the source of all truth, has said so, it's a certainty that you are blessed. You are blessed to know your heavenly Father as your creator and the preserver of your every breath. You are blessed to know Jesus Christ, His Son, the face of God's love come to earth to assure you of forgiveness, healing, and salvation. You are blessed to know the Holy Spirit, the comforter who dwells in your heart to keep you in your God-secured relationship with Him now and throughout eternity.

Allow yourself time each day to savor the truth of God's love for you. In His love, you have access to everything He has promised His people, including comfort in times of sorrow, hope in times of loss, endurance in times of hardship, and faithfulness in times of doubt. All these things are far from wispy wishes that may or may not come true! They're the essence of truth, spoken by your loving God to you.

You belong to Him. The blessings He pours on you are your inheritance to keep now and forever.

In His Footsteps

When someone does a kindness,
It always seems to me
That's the way God up in heaven
Would like us all to be.
For when we bring some pleasure
To another human heart,
We have followed in His footsteps
And we've had a little part
In serving God who loves us
For I'm very sure it's true
That in serving those around us,
We serve and please God, too.

~HSR

The Service of Love

Serve one another in love.

GALATIANS 5:13 NIV

It was such a little thing to you, but it meant so much to someone else. Perhaps you offered a friendly smile to a sales associate who had just finished with a demanding customer, or you assisted a young woman with her groceries, not knowing she had heard devastating news only hours before. Then you came along. Like a ray of sunshine, you were a bright spot in their day.

The little things you do may not seem like much, but they're as welcome, as necessary, and as courageous as the heroic deeds that make the headlines. In fact, your little acts of kindness may be even more welcome, necessary, and courageous than heroic deeds. Though there are many daily opportunities to offer help and provide encouragement to others, many people are simply too busy to care. When you stop for the sake of someone else, it's noticed.

All those little things are noticed by God, too. His Spirit is the source of your willingness and power to serve others simply and quietly, following in His footsteps, sharing His love. No, what you do may never make the headlines, but unlike today's big story that will be old news tomorrow, your little acts of kindness touch lives today, and will live in the hearts you touch forever.

Celebrating
God's Love
through Prayer

The Heavenly Staircase

Prayers are the stairs that lead to God,
And there's joy every step of the way
When we make our pilgrimage to Him
With love in our hearts each day.

~HSR

The Heart of Prayer

Pray all the time.

1 THESSALONIANS 5:17 MSG

When a prayer permeates your heart, prayer stays with you wherever you go. All day long, it's as if you're having a continuing conversation with God!

Suppose you step outside today, and you're greeted by the cheerful chirps of birds singing high in the trees. "Thank You, God!" you might say with a smile. "Thank You for the green, leafy tree and for the birds that make their nests in its branches." Or suppose you're touched by a visit from a friend who dropped by just to see how you were doing. "Thank You, God," might be the response that comes to your lips, "for putting this kind and thoughtful person into my life."

Your heart's prayer can be short, perhaps only a few words uttered from deep within the soul. It can be an exclamation of happy surprise, heartwarming gladness, or humble thanksgiving to God as you receive and appreciate His good gifts throughout the day. It can be a spontaneous remark as you share with God something you have noticed and would like to share with Him.

Truly, your heart's prayer can be as easy and as natural as saying hi to your very best friend—and after all, isn't that exactly what you're doing?

Begin Each Day by Kneeling to Pray

Start every day with a "good morning" prayer
And God will bless each thing you do
and keep you in His care...
And never, never sever the
spirit's silken strand
That our Father up in heaven
holds in His mighty hand.

~HSR

The Priority of Love

Every morning I pray to you.

PSALM 88:13 NCV

"Start your day off right!" Then the advertiser presents his product—a box of breakfast cereal, a carton of fruit juice, or a brand of daily vitamins. All these things come with the promise to help you keep your energy up throughout the day.

As important to your health as a nutritious breakfast may be, there's something even more important, and that's prayer. As soon as you wake up in the morning, take a few minutes to thank God for keeping you during the dark hours of night, and praise Him for the gift of a new day.

Beginning your day with prayer starts you off in the right direction, and that is with your heart and mind on God and His work in your life. During the day, your spiritual energy won't fade away, and you'll have God-given vitality to meet any problems or troubles that might come along.

A day begun with prayer is like a day begun with a good breakfast. One feeds the body and keeps it functioning to its fullest. The other nourishes the soul and keeps it close in touch with God, the giver of your time and abilities, the creator of the world around you.

Start every day off right. Begin with prayer!

On the Wings of Prayer

On the wings of prayer our burdens take flight
And our load of care becomes bearably light
And our heavy hearts are lifted above
To be healed by the balm of God's wonderful love. . .
And the tears in our eyes are dried by the hands
Of a loving Father who understands
All of our problems, our fears and despair
When we take them to Him on the wings of prayer.

~HSR

The Measure of Love

Devote yourselves to prayer,
being watchful and thankful.

COLOSSIANS 4:2 NIV

Surely there is no blessing God has placed in your life that you would think of as too small or too ordinary to warrant your thanks. With a heart of gratitude, you thank Him for everything! In the same way, there is no problem too small or too ordinary that you cannot take to Him in prayer.

By comparison to serious problems and life-threatening situations, your present worry may indeed seem of little consequence. Yet if it causes you concern, it's important enough to take to God in prayer.

Like a loving parent, God wants to hear you talk about what's on your mind. It doesn't need to be something earth-shattering! It's just that when He sees your downcast eyes and your drooping shoulders, He wants to hear you tell Him what's wrong, and He wants you to rely on Him to hear you and care about what you have to say.

God invites you to bring all your cares to Him, both the big ones and the small ones, the extraordinary ones and the routine ones. Anything that makes you feel anxious, any issue that burdens your heart, any fear that shadows your day is just the right size to talk over with your Father in heaven.

No Prayer Goes Unheard

Often we pause and wonder when
we kneel down to pray
Can God really hear the prayers that we say?
But if we keep praying and talking to Him,
He'll brighten the soul that
was clouded and dim.
And as we continue, our burden seems lighter,
Our sorrow is softened and
our outlook is brighter.
For though we feel helpless
and alone when we start,
A prayer is the key that opens the heart,
And as the heart opens, the dear Lord comes in
And the prayer that we felt
we could never begin
Is so easy to say, for the Lord understands
And He gives us new strength by
the touch of His hands.

~HSR

The Spirit of Prayer

Pray in the Spirit at all times with all kinds of prayers,
asking for everything you need.

EPHESIANS 6:18 NCV

Does God hear our prayers? In all likelihood, every one of us has asked that question at some point in our lives. The answer we choose is a matter of utmost importance, second only to how we reach that answer.

Prayer is a privilege we have because of the relationship we possess with God through the working of His Spirit in our hearts. We can't pray without the power of God's Spirit, and neither can we believe that God hears our prayers without the faith His Spirit nurtures in us. That is why, when we wonder whether or not God hears us when we pray, the only way we can reach a firm and trusting "yes" is with and through His Holy Spirit.

Spirit-led prayer praises and thanks God for all He has done, freely confesses sin, and receives in certainty God's forgiveness. In addition, Spirit-led prayer places all petitions and desires before God, under His will, and according to His purpose in our lives.

How sure are you that your heavenly Father hears your prayers? God yearns for you to firmly believe He hears your every word and listens with heartfelt concern and compassion. Pray for His Spirit, so you may speak to God with the boldness and confidence God desires for you!

Daily Prayers Dissolve Your Cares

I meet God in the morning and go with Him through the day,
Then in the stillness of the night before sleep comes I pray
That God will just take over all the problems I couldn't solve,
And in the peacefulness of sleep my cares will all dissolve.
So when I open up my eyes to greet another day,
I'll find myself renewed in strength and there will open up a way
To meet what seemed impossible for me to solve alone,
And once again I'll be assured I am never on my own.

~HSR

The Refreshment of Love

*If you lie down, you will not be afraid;
when you lie down, your sleep will be sweet.*

PROVERBS 3:24 ESV

"Let's sleep on it, then we can decide." We say this when we want time to think over our options and choose how to handle the problem. In reality, getting a good night's sleep helps us come back to the problem with a fresh perspective, and very often we find that the best solution is staring us right in the face!

If you kneel down before you go to bed and give the day's problems to God, you will get a good night's sleep. With the weight of your burden lifted from your mind, there's no tossing and turning, no nagging and niggling worries keeping you awake throughout the hours of darkness. There's only what God desires for you, and that's a quiet, peaceful night.

In the morning, the problem may not have changed, but you will have. Refreshed, you may find the problem isn't as frightening as you thought it was, and you have the resources to surmount it. Or you may wake with the solution clearly in your mind, as if it came straight from heaven! And who's to say it didn't?

"Let's sleep on it" is more than a figure of speech. When you add prayer to the mix, you can say Amen and leave the rest to God. Sweet dreams!

"Thy Will Be Done"

God did not promise sun without rain,
Light without darkness or joy without pain.
He only promised strength for the day
When the darkness comes and we lose our way...
For only through sorrow do we grow more aware
That God is our refuge in times of despair,
For when we are happy and life's bright and fair,
We often forget to kneel down in prayer...
But God seems much closer and needed much more
When trouble and sorrow stand outside our door,
For then we seek shelter in His wondrous love,
And we ask Him to send us help from above...
And that is the reason we know it is true
That bright, shining hours and dark, sad ones, too,
Are part of the plan God made for each one,
And all we can pray is "Thy will be done."
And know that you are never alone
For God is your Father and you're one of His own.

~HSR

The Words of Love

If you believe, you will receive whatever you ask for in prayer.

MATTHEW 21:22 NIV

Some of the most difficult words to pray and really mean what we say are "Thy will be done." Yet these are the words God directs us to add when we make our requests to Him in prayer.

In saying "Thy will be done," we remind ourselves that God is in control. We're recognizing His authority over our lives, and accepting with humility our limited human perspective and reasoning. After all, God can see the big picture, while we're looking at only a small part of it. God knows more than we do what's best for us, and He knows how to lead and guide us according to His purpose.

In His love for you, God invites you to tell Him your deepest desires, and to ask Him for those things you long for and hope to receive. He wants you to dream and imagine, to work and reach, to see and pursue the opportunities all around you. He listens to your words and He receives them with gladness; and He waits for these words of surrender to flow from your heart: "Thy will be done."

God's purpose, though it may appear unfathomable to you right now, always works to the good over time. Let His sovereign will remain your genuine and ultimate request in every prayer.

A Special Prayer for You

I said a special prayer for you—I asked the Lord above
To keep you safely in His care and enfold you in His love.
I did not ask for fortune, for riches or for fame,
I only asked for blessings in the Holy Savior's name—
Blessings to surround you in times of trial and stress,
And inner joy to fill your heart with peace and happiness.

~HSR

The Prayer of Love

*I tell you to pray for all people, asking God for
what they need and being thankful to him.*

1 TIMOTHY 2:1 NCV

When a loved one suffers, we're often at a loss to know how to
help. We wish we could take away the pain, but we can't. We long
to do something to make things right again, to put things back
the way they used to be, but we don't have the power, and we
know it.

God, in His compassion for our human limitations, has
given us the privilege of praying on behalf of others. Just as
we are invited to lift up our burdens to Him, we may also lift
up the names of those who are suffering and set their needs in
front of His divine throne. He has promised to hear, and He
has promised to act in His own time and according to His will.

When you pray for others, you join your voice with all
believers who, out of love, pray for the needs of the world. Your
prayers bless your loved ones in a way you may never know this
side of heaven, but you can be certain your prayers are working
for the good of those whose names rest on your heart.

God has given you the power to do the most thoughtful
and most loving thing you can do for anyone. God has given
you the power to pray.

The Mystery of Prayer

Beyond that which words can
interpret or theology explain,
The soul feels a shower of refreshment
that falls like the gentle rain
On hearts that are parched with problems
and are searching to find the way
To somehow attract God's attention
through well-chosen words as they pray,
Not knowing that God in His wisdom
can sense all man's worry and woe,
For there is nothing man can conceal
that God does not already know. . .
So kneel in prayer in His presence
and you'll find no need to speak,
For softly in quiet communion,
God grants you the peace that you seek.

~HSR

The Utterance of Love

The Spirit himself speaks to God for us, even begs God for us with deep feelings that words cannot explain.
ROMANS 8:26 NCV

Sometimes words fail us. We don't know what to say to a friend who has suffered an untimely loss, nor to a child who has been traumatized by events beyond her understanding. All we can do is reach out and offer our silent but heartfelt companionship at a time of intense sorrow.

In prayer, too, there are times when words cannot begin to express our feelings. Perhaps we're in a state of pain and confusion, and we don't even know what to pray for. This is when God sends His Holy Spirit to pray on our behalf.

From the depth of our hearts, God's Spirit carries to our heavenly Father the pain we haven't the power to put into words, the anguish known only to ourselves alone. The Holy Spirit takes all these things to the foot of God's throne and asks God for the healing He knows we need.

When the words you so desperately want to say just aren't there for you, rely on the Holy Spirit's help and guidance. Relax, breathe deeply, and remain in prayerful silence, giving over to God's Spirit to do what you cannot. Trust in Him to pour on you the soothing balm of God's love and fill your soul with His peace.

A Word from the Author Just for You

I am only a worker employed by the Lord,
And great is my gladness and rich my reward
If I can just spread the wonderful story
That God is the answer to eternal glory. . .
And only the people who read my poems
Can help me to reach more hearts and homes,
Bringing new hope and comfort and cheer,
Telling sad hearts there is nothing to fear,
And what greater joy could there be than to share
The love of God and the power of prayer.

~HSR

The Aid of Love

*The prayer of a righteous person has
great power as it is working.*

JAMES 5:16 ESV

A young boy fell off his bicycle and hurt himself. Although several adults saw what happened, no one lifted a finger to help the boy get up, and no one offered to wipe and bandage his scrapes. We would be angry to hear of such a thing happening in our community!

Spiritually, we often act like those uncaring adults. There have been times when our loved ones were anxious, fearful, or troubled in spirit, but we neglected to share with them the power of prayer. We recall the names of those who have asked us to pray for them, and realize we have forgotten to do so. We know we have walked away instead of spending a few minutes praying with those who have needed someone to guide them to God.

Our Savior Jesus has taken these sins and all other sins to the cross, saving us from the consequences of God's righteous anger. With our repentance, God's Spirit helps us share the power of prayer with a hurting world.

Today, pray for all those who have fallen and have no one to help them get up. Pray for the Holy Spirit to open your eyes to the spiritual wounds of others and to enable you to comfort them in the arms of heartfelt prayer.

*Celebrating
God's Love
through Meditation*

Good Morning, God

You are ushering in another day, untouched and freshly new,
So here I am to ask You, God, if You'll renew me, too. . .
Forgive the many errors that I made yesterday
And let me try again, dear God, to walk closer in Thy way. . .
But, Father, I am well aware I can't make it on my own,
So take my hand and hold it tight for I can't walk alone.

~HSR

The Renewal of Love

As far as the east is from the west,
so far has he removed our transgressions from us.

PSALM 103:12 NKJV

To remain healthy, our bodies require a certain number of hours of sleep. When we have a short night, we feel it! Fatigue follows us from morning to evening, and we aren't at our best all day.

Much as the bodies need sleep, our souls need forgiveness even more. Without forgiveness, we will never feel at ease with ourselves, with others, or with God. It will be impossible to live at our spiritual best.

Forgiveness comes when we humbly acknowledge our sins and admit our weaknesses before God, believing in His desire and ability to grant us forgiveness. No matter what weighs on our mind, once confessed and forgiven, God promises to lift it off our soul and never look at it again. Placing faith in His pardon is like waking up in the morning after a sound, restful sleep—we're refreshed and renewed, and we're feeling like a million dollars!

God intends for you to come to Him whenever you are fatigued with guilt or tired of hiding from something that causes you sleepless nights and anxious days. Ask His forgiveness, then meditate on the miracle of the innocence and purity you have in His sight.

Because God gave His best to you in Jesus, you can live at your best today and every day of your life.

Inspiration! Meditation! Dedication!

Brighten your day
And lighten your way
And lessen your cares
With daily prayers.
Quiet your mind
And leave tension behind
And find inspiration
In hushed meditation.

~HSR

The Attentiveness of Love

I will meditate on all your works and
consider all your mighty deeds.

Psalm 77:12 niv

When someone you're speaking with is easily distracted, you might find it hard to keep the conversation on track. In fact, you might give up in frustration!

When we set aside time to be alone with God, we're often like the easily distracted person. Our thoughts flit from one subject to another. Something catches our eye, a memory pops into mind, a sound grabs our attention—all this can happen in the space of only a few minutes' time. It's no wonder we feel scattered and distracted, and it's not surprising that many of us believe we're unable to meditate.

Meditation is simply the act of quieting your mind and focusing on one thing—the conversation God desires to have with you through the words of scripture. When you are mindful of His presence and attentive to His promises, God fills your soul with His wisdom and His peace. He deepens your faith, gives you insight, and strengthens your understanding of His will and purpose for your life.

Today, spend a few minutes focused on one thought about God or on a passage of scripture. If your mind strays, gently pull it back again. Do this every day, slowly increasing the time you meditate. Give Him your full attention, because you indeed have His.

The Peace of Meditation

So we may know God better and feel His quiet power,
Let us daily keep in silence a meditation hour. . .
For to understand God's greatness and to use His gifts each day,
The soul must learn to meet Him in a meditative way. . .
For our Father tells His children that if they would know His will
They must seek Him in the silence when all is calm and still. . .
For nature's great forces are found in quiet things
Like softly falling snowflakes drifting down on angels' wings
Or petals dropping soundlessly from a lovely full-blown rose,
So God comes closest to us when our souls are in repose. . .
So let us plan with prayerful care to always allocate
A certain portion of each day to be still and meditate. . .
For when everything is quiet and we're lost in meditation,
Our souls are then preparing for a deeper dedication
That will make it wholly possible to quietly endure
The violent world around us, for in God we are secure.

~HSR

The Serenity of Love

After the earthquake fire, but God wasn't in the fire;
and after the fire a gentle and quiet whisper.
1 KINGS 19:12 MSG

We're accustomed to being surrounded by noise—by voices and tunes, by ringtones and beeps, by motors and horns. Though noise is an integral part of the modern world we live in day in and day out, noise can drown out the softer sounds and gentle whispers that draw us closer to God.

Just as important as taking time out to meditate on God's presence in your life is to take the noise out, too. First, turn off your phone, TV, radio, and computer so you will not be disturbed. Second, find a time when other members of your family are unlikely to interrupt you, and let them know you would like to spend, say, a half hour by yourself. Third, go to a place where you can sit quietly and at peace. For some, it's by a window; for others, it's outdoors in a garden or park.

In the stillness, you will begin noticing things, like the rhythmic swish of a breeze rustling the leaves, the murmur of distant thunder, the hum of a bee nestled in the sweet nectar of a flower. In the sanctuary of your soul, you will hear the whisper of God's voice as He enfolds you in His peace, a peace no outside noise can penetrate or ever take away.

I Come to Meet You

I come to meet You, God, and as I linger here
I seem to feel You very near.
A rustling leaf, a rolling slope
Speak to my heart of endless hope.
The sun just rising in the sky,
The waking birdlings as they fly,
The grass all wet with morning dew
Are telling me I just met You. . .
And gently thus the day is born
As night gives way to breaking morn,
And once again I've met You, God,
And worshipped on Your holy sod. . .
For who could see the dawn break through
Without a glimpse of heaven and You?
For who but God could make the day
And softly put the night away?

~HSR

The Awareness of Love

I beg you to reaffirm your love for him.

2 CORINTHIANS 2:8 ESV

Have you ever learned later that someone did you a kindness? Perhaps a family friend praised your cooking skills to others, or recommended you for a coveted position; or maybe a neighbor kindly picked up some branches that had fallen in your yard. When you became aware of what the person did, you offered your sincerest thanks.

God has done and continues to do so much for us, yet many of us remain unaware of Him as the source of our daily blessings and the many kindnesses we receive from His hand. We fail to acknowledge the eternal favor God did for us when He sent His Son Jesus to take upon himself the consequences of our sin. Willingly and unselfishly, Jesus died so we could know forgiveness, and He rose again so we could share in His victory over death.

Long ago, Jesus did you a kindness no one else could have done—He brought you into relationship with your heavenly Father, and made it possible for you to live a life of spiritual awareness and joy-filled gratitude.

Are you conscious of all the kindnesses your God has done for you? Take time now to meditate on all the ways God has worked in your life and all the ways He continues to show His love for you.

A Part of Me

Dear God, You are a part of me—
You're all I do and all I see,
You're what I say and what I do,
For all my life belongs to You.
You walk with me and talk with me,
For I am Yours eternally,
And when I stumble, slip, and fall
Because I'm weak and lost and small,
You help me up and take my hand
And lead me toward the Promised Land.
I cannot dwell apart from You—
You would not ask or want me to,
For You have room within Your heart
To make each child of Yours a part
Of You and all Your love and care
If we but come to You in prayer.

~HSR

A Special Prayer

Heavenly Father, thank You for all the ways You show Your
love for me, and for all the blessings You have poured out on
my life. Remain beside me, Lord, in every step I take, and fill
my heart with boundless love for You. Amen.